NO WILL OF MY OWN

How Patriarchy Smothers
Female Dignity & Personhood

By **Jon Zens**

Ekklesia Press, 2011

No Will Of My Own
How Patriarchy Smothers Female Dignity & Personhood

Library of Congress Control Number 2011923484

Publisher's Cataloging-in-Publication data

Zens, Jon.
   No will of my own : how patriarchy smothers female dignity and personhood / by Jon Zens.
    p. cm.
    ISBN 978-0-9827446-3-5
    Includes bibliographical references.
1. Patriarchy--Religious aspects--Christianity. 2. Patriarchy--Religious aspects--Catholic Church. 3. Violence --Religious aspects --Christianity. 4. Equality --Religious aspects --Christianity. 5. Women in Christianity. 6. Women --Biblical teaching. I. Title.

BV639.W7.Z46 2011
270.8/3/082 dc22
2011923484

Cover Design: Ralph Polendo
Cover Art: Kathy Huff © 2011
Back Cover Image: *Broken Girl*, Jessica Braddock-Gavit © 2000

Material from *Christianity and Incest* by Annie Fransen Imbens and Ineke De Putter Jonker, translated by P. McVay copyright © 1992 Fortress Press. Reproduced by permission of Augsburg Fortress Publishers.

Omaha, NE

TABLE OF CONTENTS:

DEDICATED TO

Kristy Childs
(Veronica's Voice, Kansas City)

—and—

Trisha Baptie
(Honour Ministries, Vancouver, B.C.)

Both are shining trophies of Jesus' grace,
survivors of untold horrors and helpers of
those still stuck in the sex trade.

FOREWORD

I am embarrassed to write the foreword for this excellent little book by my friend Jon Zens for a couple of reasons. First, the person who should be writing it is Paulo Fuller in the Philippines. Paulo serves as the Director of *Renew Foundation*, a ministry devoted to help women and children escape the sex trade in Angeles City. Unfortunately, due to Paulo's non-stop work in Angeles City, he just does not have the time to write this Foreword. Jon Zens' wife, Dotty, and Bonnie Jaeckle from the United States are assisting Paulo in Filipino bar/ street ministry for four weeks in early 2011. Paulo is far more qualified than I to talk about *No Will of My Own*. I am a pastor who understands intuitively and theologically the problems associated with patriarchy, but Paulo is on the streets and understands them experientially. For those of you who may doubt the connection Jon makes between patriarchy and sexual sins behind the closed doors of Christian homes, Paulo's ministry and the dozens of others like it can sadly confirm what Jon writes. Many of the girls who wind up in the sex trade come from patriarchal homes.

Second, the content of this book is not easy to read. What Jon writes is important to read and understand, but it will not be comfortable to digest. Were it not for the false belief system that serves as the underpinning of patriarchy, there would be no need for this book to exist.

Patriarchy is the belief that men have complete authority in the home, and that husbands should rule over their wives and children. Most conservative Christians who advocate patriarchy base their views on what God told Eve when she rebelled and God, pronouncing judgment on Eve, said:

> I will surely multiply your pain in childbearing; in pain you shall bring forth children. *Your desire shall be for your husband, and he shall rule over you*, (Genesis 3:16).

Patriarchalists say that the last portion of Genesis 3:16 means that (1) God commands that a woman should display sexual desire for her man (i.e., "*your desire shall be for your husband*"), and that (2) The male is to be the head, authority and ruler over the women in his home (i.e., "*and he shall rule over you*"). Women should be subservient to the men, and the Christian home ought to be governed by men, because God commands it to be that way, say those Christians who hold to patriarchy.

However, using basic principles of interpretation, one can easily see Genesis 3:16 spells out the consequences of sin and is not a commandment from God. The woman's desire for her husband in Genesis 3:16 is not, at least linguistically and contextually, a sexual desire. The word translated "desire" (*teshuqah*) is used in the next chapter, Genesis 4:7, where *teshuqah* refers to sin's desire to *control* Cain. Thus, letting the Bible interpret itself, the word "desire" in both Genesis 3:16 and Genesis 4:7 means "a desire to control."

Simply put, sin causes a desire to dominate or control. The curse of sin becomes a constant battle for control. *This is not how God created relationships between men and women to be.* Many conservative Christians, though, have made the mistake of interpreting Genesis 3:16 to teach that God commands the woman to stay home, give sexual fulfillment to her man, while God has given the man complete authority to control and govern the women in his life. This theology of male domination can, left unchecked, provide an atmosphere for deeper abuse to take place.

When the God of all grace, however, gets a grip on the home, no longer will there be a fight to see who dominates and controls the other. Rather, there will be mutual submission between the husband and the wife because there is mutual equality (i.e., Ephesians 5:21 – "*submitting to one another in reverence to Christ*"). Mutual submission, with no thought of control, is God's design for the home. It should be the effort of every Bible-believing church, pastor and teacher to instruct husbands and wives on the sinful nature of any husband or wife who seeks to dominate the home.

Dr. Richard Hess, Professor of Old Testament and Semitic Languages at Denver Theological Seminary comments on Genesis 3:16. Dr. Hess said all Christians should attempt to pull down any patriarchal system of domination and control in the Christian home, and then responds to those who object to any attempt to end patriarchy:

It is no more a sin to end this consequence of the fall than it is to use weed killer to end the promised weeds and thorns in the following verses. No, the emphasis [in Genesis 3:16] is on the terrible effects of sin, and the destruction of a harmonious relationship that once existed. In its place comes a harmful struggle of wills.

In *No Will of My Own*, author Jon Zens gives evidence of how patriarchy's warped view of male dominance can lead females to the dark place of having no will of their own. My prayer is that pastors and Christian people will read this book and find help to resist any involvement in the patriarchal movement that purports to be from God but gives experiential evidence to the contrary.

Pastor Wade Burleson
Emmanuel Baptist Church
Enid, Oklahoma, January, 2011

INTRODUCTION

Interaction with *Christianity & Incest*
[hereafter, *CAI*]
by Annie Imbens and Ineke Jonker,
Fortress Press, 1992, 298 pages

"Home-schooled girls do not need 'further' education; they should just prepare for being a wife and mother." "A daughter should stay at home and serve her father until he chooses a husband for her." "The daughter is a 'helpmeet' for her father." "Parents should never let their daughter be out of their sight." "Women should never work outside the home." These and many similar sentiments are being dogmatically expressed by leaders of the Christian Patriarchy Movement.

The home-schooling movement in America has been growing for the past forty years. The momentum of this movement spawned hundreds of national and regional home-schooling conventions and events. Among the featured speakers are some who espouse a patriarchal view of Christianity in which men and boys trump women and girls. On the tables and in the booths at such conventions will be found many books and media options espousing this viewpoint. A good summary of this movement can be found at http://www.alternet.org/reproductivejustice/149022/creepy_christian_patriarchy_movement_shackles_daughters_to_their_fathers_and_homes/. I would like to compare some of the major features of the aggressive patriarchy movement in the USA with the Netherlands-based research found in *Christianity & Incest*.

"Patriarchy" is a human social construct wherein "a woman must conform to expectations, be subservient, stay in the background, be quiet, sweet, and caring, and above all care for and serve the men" (*CAI*, p.138). Further, "girls are trained to take a back seat to boys. Boys and girls are brought up in such a way that men's power over women remains intact" (*CAI*, p.239). "The basic premise [of patriarchy] is that women are inferior to men and that women should therefore obey men" (*CAI*, p.275).

In the 1980's Annie Imbens and Ineke Jonker began research with survivors of incest in the Netherlands who came from Roman Catholic and Dutch Reformed upbringings. Their findings were first published in Dutch in 1985, and the third edition appeared in 1991. In 1992 a 298-page English translation, *Christianity & Incest* [*CAI*], was published by Fortress Press.

This book powerfully exposes the severe ill-effects of church or religious authority-based patriarchy on women. Obviously, any human system will have a wide range of manifestations among those within its pale. In this case, incest is the extreme at one end of the spectrum (*CAI*, p.151), while non-sexual forms of female suppression lie at the other (*CAI*, p.207). *CAI* focuses on incest, but by putting the worst extreme under the magnifying glass, the negative attributes in patriarchy that affect all females are thereby exposed.

Let me be clear that I am not opposed to home-schooling. My three children experienced alternative forms of education, including home-schooling. I am, however, very concerned about the bondage of females that is connected to the legalistic practice of the vocal patriarchal wing of the home-schooling movement in America.

Jon Zens
March 2011

REALITY AS
CONSTRUCTED BY MEN

Sadly, the visible church has been shaped and dominated by males because the primary players have always been men. Women were systematically removed from the church's story, and marginalized in church functions (*cf.* Anne Jensen, *God's Self-Confident Daughters: Early Christianity & the Liberation of Women*, Westminster John Knox, 1996). "Traditional theology...examines reality primarily from the standpoint of the experiences and insights of men" (*CAI*, p.287; *cf. Sexism: The Male Monopoly on History & Thought*, Farrar/Straus/Giroux, 1982).

These facts are all the more significant as we consider how the church has treated women in its practice (Garry Wills, "Excluded Women," *Papal Sin: Structures of Deceit*, Doubleday, 2000, pp.104-121).

ABUSE OCCURS IN STRICT RELIGIOUS HOMES

"Why is it," the authors ask, "that a relatively high number of children who are sexually abused by men within the family come from very strict religious families?" (*CAI*, p.7) Based on their studies they conclude that "the sexual abuse of girls within the family [is] the ultimate consequence of patriarchal thinking, of patriarchal theology, and of the patriarchal experience of Christianity" (p.3). The following are some key reasons why patriarchy and the humiliation of women go hand in hand.

PATRIARCHY CREATES AN ATMOSPHERE WHERE ABUSE CAN FLOURISH

Great pressure is put upon girls in many Christian homes to be passive and submissive in extraordinarily unhealthy ways. Bible themes are interpreted in a manner giving the impression to a young lady that she can only honor God by doing whatever her father says.

> The most important message a woman hears in church is *obedience*. Eve was disobedient and that's why sin came into the world. A daughter sees this obedience in Mother, with whom she identifies herself. She must honor her father and mother....A woman must keep silent. That was quite normal in the church. A girl has to stay in the background, is not allowed to be an altar "boy." She must love her neighbor and be self-sacrificing....She learned

from the Bible that she is the property of men, someone "in relation to others" (*CAI*, p.140).

Teaching of this sort stereotypes girls so they feel they must give in to whatever their fathers or other male authority figures desire of them.

BOYS ARE MORE IMPORTANT

The tone that pervades the [Old Testament] and the Talmud, however, is not very different from that which runs through the literature of other nations, showing that woman was held of less account than man. The Mishna speaks of him who prays that his wife may bring forth a son rather than a daughter. In Hebrew law women were not competent witnesses either in civil or in criminal cases (Lewis N. Dembitz, "Woman," *The Jewish Encyclopedia*, Vol. XII, Funk & Wagnalls, 1907, p.557).

Patriarchy openly communicates to females in their family-life that *boys take precedence over girls in all things*. Incest survivors observed in their families, "Boys are a better breed. Good fathers have sons, and fatherhood means putting more sons on the earth.... Father thinks boys are more important. He says so: 'Good men father sons'" (*CAI*, pp.76, 123). "The patriarchal ideology of motherhood" avers "that it is her purpose to produce children, preferably male heirs" (*CAI*, p.120). "The man is the central figure as the procreator of (preferably) male descendents" (*CAI*, p.166).

Years ago I heard a cassette tape put out by the Plymouth Foundation in which the speaker said at least four times, "When you fathers train your sons...." He never mentioned the daughters in that room. It was as if only the sons counted.

WOMEN ARE ASSOCIATED WITH EVIL

In patriarchy women are blamed, without exception. "The woman is always the symbol of evil and weakness" (*CAI*, p.59). "In essence, women are weak, seductive, sinful, and untrustworthy" (*CAI*, p.257). When it comes to sexual misconduct, "it is the woman who gets the ball rolling, they said" (*CAI*, p.59).

"My brother," one survivor recalled, "looked under my girlfriend's skirt once. When I said something to him about it, he replied, 'Then she shouldn't sit like that'" (*CAI*, p.76).

Modesty is a high priority in the Christian patriarchy movement, but it always places the bulk of the responsibility on the women rather than on the men. If there is a lapse in morality, the girl will likely be blamed as the cause.

"HONOR YOUR FATHER & MOTHER" PERVERTED

The commandment to honor one's parents becomes in patriarchy an open license for males to violate females in the family, not only incestuously but in demanding the complicity of women for violations of other females. "Crying about or resisting sexual abuse by Father is seen as rebellion against Father ('defying Father'), therefore sinful, and as rebellion against or defying God….When they dared to ask the offender questions about it, they were told that all fathers do that, that it was good for them, or that they themselves had given cause because they were seductive and evil, just like Eve….They honored their fathers and mothers, despite the sexual abuse by their fathers" (*CAI*, pp.194-195).

"When survivors resisted, they are also bad because they are disobedient, rebelling against men and the natural order created by God, in which women are intended to be subservient to men, and children obedient to parents" (*CAI*, p.217).

The use of Scripture by adults can become a very tricky exercise. It is clear that the Lord wants parents to be properly honored. Children are instructed to "obey" their parents in the Lord. But it can become a convenient thing for fathers to use these Biblical themes to threaten, intimidate, manipulate, and control children. A child's mind can begin to grasp the concept of "obeying" as taught by adults, but things can become very fuzzy and confusing when the "obedience" called for feels instinctively wrong to the youth. It is a very grave aberration for a mom or dad to use "obey your parents" as a means to fulfill their self-centered agendas.

Through me, my children and others are supposed to understand God better. Even if they reject what they understand.

ACTIVE CHURCH MEN
TERRORIZE GIRLS AT HOME

Armed with such twisted notions of "submission" and "honor your father," the patriarchal ideology creates a context in which young girls can be violated with impunity by male family members.

Fathers, brothers, grandfathers, and uncles who, with a prayerbook or collection plate in one hand [can] molest their daughters, sisters, granddaughters, and nieces with the other (Nel Draijer, "Foreword," *CAI*, p.xii)....Offenders used Bible passages or church-authorized texts in order to be able to abuse girls and keep them quiet about it....The most astounding realization is that these girls in Christian families have had experiences comparable to those undergone by people in concentration camps. The offenders were decent, well-functioning adults in the community, sometimes with highly respected professions. With the exception of one, all of the women interviewed have turned their backs on the church. The majority of the offenders, however, are still involved in the church. Half of them still occupy an official church position (Annie Imbens, "Authors' Prefaces," *CAI*, p.xvi).

It is frightening to consider how much sexual abuse is perpetrated by church leaders. The following internet resources give some indication of the extent of this sickening problem: http://www.reformation.com/CSA/allabuse.html; also see: http://dannimoss.wordpress.com/2008/06/20/protestant-clergy-abuse-equals-or-exceeds-catholic-clergy-abuse/; http://www.stopbaptistpredators.org/article07/child_sex_abuse_by_protestant_clergy.html.

AFTER ABUSE TAKES PLACE, FEMALES ARE DEEPLY WOUNDED FURTHER BECAUSE:

Girls are taught to believe that they provoked their own abuse. "When these survivors, who are sweet, obedient, and subservient to men or boys, are sexually abused by them, they are blamed for the abuse because they are seductive – that's just the way women are" (*CAI*, p.217). One survivor commented, "He was very crafty, too. I knew that if I said anything about it, he'd say, 'You wanted it too'" (*CAI*, p.28).

Girls are taught to take the blame for their own abuse. "It always came down to the same thing: the girl was the one to blame" (*CAI*, p.63).

Matriarchy – just as damaging

"Sometimes I asked my father," said one survivor, "why he kept making me do this. Then he said, 'All women are the same as that first woman, Eve. You tempt me. In your heart, this is what you want, just like Eve.'" (*CAI*, p.66). She goes on to say, "The incest was my fault, I kept thinking. I wanted to kill myself....The atmosphere at home [was one] of terror. I've thought about that a lot. The oppressive side of religion, the predetermined role for women. It's always their fault. Theology validates that" (*CAI*, p.74). "The entire problem rests on the woman's shoulders" (*CAI*, p.161).

The Botkin sisters, speaking for the Christian patriarchy movement, affirm that women are responsible for the state of the men around them. They essentially tell the daughters that they are accountable for the success or failure of the males in their lives (www.visionarydaughters.com).

If girls speak about the abuse, they are not taken seriously. In the patriarchal setting, "the words of fathers and older brothers...carry more weight than the words of girls" (*CAI*, p.4). As was noted above, males are more important than females, and thus "the words of incest survivors carried less weight than those of their brothers ('Go ahead and scream; they won't believe you, anyway')" (*CAI*, p.21).

When girls who had been repeatedly raped mustered up enough courage to talk about their abuse to mothers, grandmothers and church leaders, they were met with deaf ears, or excuses were made for the offenders. During their research the authors discovered "how difficult it is for male members of the clergy to consider seriously what women say and feel" (*CAI*, p.54).

Abused girls cannot pursue and reflect on life for themselves. When one survivor was being interviewed, she "kept telling us what her father (the offender) thought and felt. She found it difficult to say what she herself thought about guilt and about various Bible passages" (*CAI*, p.12). Another survivor "internalized her grandpa's ideas about women" (*CAI*, p.34). One of the most horrendous results of incest is that the survivors "have learned to see reality through the eyes of the offender" (*CAI*, p.280). Further, because the father is associated with religion and uses the Bible to legitimate the violation of his daughter, "she identified God with the offender" (*CAI*, pp.143, 281).

"Integral to Vision Forum's belief about female submission is making sure that women are not independent at any point in their lives, regardless of age; hence the organization's enthusiasm

We will see things thru some sort of filter, prism, God's or Satan's.

for stay-at-home daughterhood" (newsfeed.time. com/2010/12/08/meet-the-selfless-women-of-the-stay-at-home-daughters-movement). Stacy McDonald and others have encouraged young women to always be accompanied by an adult when out of the home, and some do not allow daughters to even get a driver's license, stating that a future husband might not approve of his wife driving.

While boys are given the freedom to pursue many career choices, daughters are given "the tools for dominion," that is, kitchen and homemaking supplies. Many home-schooled girls are not taught academics beyond the eighth grade, stressing instruction in the domestic arts instead, since preparing them otherwise might lead them to seek higher education or to work outside the home.

The offenders are excused. While the offender gives his sob story to the professionals—"I'm sorry; I won't do it again; she seduced me; I have problems at work"—"the survivor sits alone in her room. No one bothers about her. She is inconsequential to the church until she comes to ask for forgiveness" (*CAI*, p.163). "The criminals remain members [of the church], while the survivors—who have been wounded in their souls—flee the church" (*CAI*, p.164). "Thus, the oppressed person is always wrong and the powerful person is always right" (*CAI*, p.164). In the 1960s - 1980s "the professionals reinforced the offender in his pathetic behavior and minimized the survivor's story" (*CAI*, p.164).

The deep wounds and emotional scars embedded in the lives of incest survivors cannot be separated from the church teachings that contributed significantly to "theologically legitimated violence" (*CAI*, p.xv).

> The patriarchal experience of Christianity is destructive to women. Men derive from it the ability to humiliate and sexually abuse girls and women, as well as the ability to blame them for the abuse. Consequently, the innermost feelings of these women were systematically denied, negated, or raped (*CAI*, p.207).

Battle of the mind – who will control it, influence it
There is theologically legitimated discrimination.

PATRIARCHAL PRACTICE
RESULTS IN...

Young girls' boundaries being ruthlessly violated.
As the offender "slowly builds a relationship of trust
with the child," situations are created in which the
"blurring and overstepping" of boundaries takes
place (*CAI*, p.126). In patriarchy "a man is permitted
to overstep a woman's boundaries; a woman is
forbidden to overstep a man's" (*CAI*, p.141).

One female who was counseling a young woman
learned that her dad insisted on knowing the details
of his daughters' monthly cycles. A Christian
professional counselor stated that prying into such
matters would be viewed as abusive behavior.

Girls losing their personhood. Listen to these
women from Roman Catholic and Dutch Reformed
homes describe the impact of church teachings and
abuse on their lives: "I was denied as a person; I had
no will of my own; my identity was negated; I always
felt like a thing; I was told to suppress my own desires

and feelings; I was only allowed to be the way others wanted me to be; I have no say in matters; don't ask any questions; don't use your imagination" (*CAI*, pp.78, 92, 97, 99-100, 266-267). "The survivor's will is systematically suppressed, curtailed" (*CAI*, p.133). "Each woman says that she has lost her identity, and her personality, and her femaleness" (*CAI*, p.154).

"People with no identity have no language, either. She was not allowed to talk about the worst thing that ever happened to her" (*CAI*, p.156). And even if she did try to speak to some adult about it, the likelihood of being heard was almost nil.

One girl stated that her emotions were turned off at age eight. Another girl said that "inside, she had turned to stone, but on the outside she goes through life laughing" (*CAI*, pp.158-159). "Many girls are ashamed of their bodies. They move stiffly, are tense when they sit. They do not want to be touched, are later physically distant with their children, sometimes have problems making love" (*CAI*, p.178).

Such women end up feeling like a "being without a soul, a puppet on a string" (*CAI*, p.253). They are not accepted as "thinking human beings" but viewed "as an extension of their husbands and existing for the benefit of their husbands" (*CAI*, p.255).

Girls' gifts being buried. "As a woman you had to suppress certain talents; they weren't appropriate to your role in life" (*CAI*, p.87). A good mother would teach her daughter to "repress her feelings, desires and natural talents (which are not appropriate to her role), and to make these subservient to the feelings, desires and talents of men, specifically fathers and brothers" (*CAI*, p.257).

Many in the Christian patriarchy movement teach that a mom can only teach her sons until they are thirteen. After that they must be instructed by the fathers. If mothers teach boys past the age of thirteen, it is suggested that this practice might result in sons becoming homosexual.

In the Old and New Testaments the gifts of women were expressed and appreciated. As married women, both Deborah and Huldah were prophetesses and functioned freely in Israel. Under Christ in the new covenant, the first announcement from Peter's lips cited the prophet Joel concerning the prophesying of both men and women (Acts 2:16-17).

God's commandments are both conditional & unconditional - Putting other's needs first is a commandment but not not if there in need is to abuse.

GIRLS BEING DENIED THE EDUCATION THEY DESIRE

The fear than an idle wife would fall either into intrigues or melancholia shows that study or reading was not a common diversion of women (Lewis N. Dembitz, "Woman," *The Jewish Encyclopedia*, Vol. XII, 1907, p.557)

"We had a very authoritarian pastor. When my girlfriend and I were accepted at the high school for business administration, he told us that he thought it was ridiculous. He said, 'You're just going to get married later, anyway.'" (*CAI*, p.94). One father said, "Girls don't need to study because they are going to get married anyway" (*CAI*, p.123).

A contemporary home-schooling voice, Kevin Swanson, suggests that women who go to college instead of staying under their fathers' protection will end up in a "pin-stripe suit selling their flesh cheap in the market place and will have three abortions" (http://truewomanhood.wordpress.com/2007/07/19/kevin-swanson-responds-to-reactions-he-got-from-his-broadcast-with-the-botkin-sisters-karen/).

Females being silenced. "A woman must keep silent. That was quite normal in the church" (*CAI*, p.140). "From their position of power, they have determined that only men possess this ability" to order the world according to "God's will." "In so doing, they have looked after their own interests and reduced women to silence" (*CAI*, p.189). "Passages from Paul have been misused for centuries to keep women" silent (*CAI*, p.275).

THE PATRIARCHY SYSTEM HURTS ALL WOMEN AND GIRLS

"The power of men over women in the family is legitimated by Christian churches [in the words spoken by the minister, bride and groom in the Dutch Reformed wedding services]. This results in power abuse, which has negative effects of varying degrees on many Christian women married to men who put into practice the theoretical ideas on which these [Dutch Reformed] marriage services are based. This power of men over women, which receives its legitimacy from the Christian churches, is the most important factor in the sexual abuse of girls in the family" (*CAI*, p.251).

"As long as men dominate women, men have the power to use women in order to satisfy their needs and wants, to fulfill their wishes, and to make the women responsible for the consequences of the men's own behavior" (*CAI*, p.262).

"Men/husbands, unhindered by women/wives, who have been rendered powerless, can do whatever they like. Girls in Christian families are brought up in such a way that they learn to be submissive to men (fathers and brothers)....Girls are thus easily made prey to sexual abuse by male members of the immediate or extended family. They learn not to resist power abuse by men and boys. Sexual abuse of girls in the family is the ultimate consequence of male dominion of women legitimated by the church" (*CAI*, p.248).

FATHERS ARE THE CENTER OF THE HOME

"The whole family revolved around" father, one survivor observed, and "nothing was ever his fault" (*CAI*, p.106). When she told her father at age thirteen that she was pregnant by him, his first reaction was, "Oh, what am I going to do now?" He had no concern for what the daughter was going to face as a result of his abuse (*CAI*, p.109).

"Father is the authority, and his will decides" (*CAI*, p.134). "The person with the most power resources is in control....[Abusers] use power in the form of money, presents, trips, more knowledge, experience, a better vocabulary, and superior status....Adults forget that the violation of a person's boundaries is not experienced by the powerful person the same way as the weaker person: An elephant does not feel the mouse he stands on; the mouse does" (*CAI*, pp.168-169).

MOTHERS ENFORCE THE FATHER'S CONTROL

"At school, we learned that the Father represented the lawmaking system, and the Mother law enforcement" (*CAI*, p.89). "Mother maintains the patriarchal order in the family, which preserves the power of men over women" (*CAI*, p.257). "Women were charged with ensuring that, from a very young age, girls were made dependent upon men" (*CAI*, p.258). Thus, "Mothers who allowed their daughters to be abused were obedient to their husbands in all things" (*CAI*, p.256).

CONCLUDING THOUGHTS

Within patriarchy and even outside of it, fathers milk "male headship" for all it is worth. "Father had six women in the house, so he lived like a king. When he came home, his slippers were brought to him, his beer was cold, his paper was waiting, supper was served on the dot" (*CAI*, p.106). He also had an official position in a Dutch Reformed church. But while this father fooled outsiders with his friendliness, inside the home he raped his daughters and two of them were impregnated a total of three times—and many times he made the boys watch his abuse (*CAI*, p.108).

Anna Sofia and Elizabeth Botkin assert in their book, *So Much More: The Remarkable Influence of Visionary Daughters on the Kingdom of God*, that a young lady should stay at home *serving her father* until a husband is chosen for her by him. They even use the word "helpmeet"—a word in Scripture exclusively connected to the wife—to describe the daughter's relationship to her dad.

Patriarchy teaches females to be passive and non-thinking. Girls are trained to "meet the expectations and requirements men have of women." What dad says is law and "discussion is not tolerated....He makes sure he is unapproachable." "Obedient wives do not ask their husbands critical questions, do not complain, and do not show their emotions" (*CAI*, pp.256-257).

Survivors made comments like these about the values they grew up with: "Don't have any opinions of your own; Have no say in matters; Don't think; Don't ask any questions; Don't use your imagination; I was to be seen and not heard" (*CAI*, pp.265-267).

How can a woman under the thumb of patriarchy say to the Lord, "not my will but yours," and "not my life but yours" when she has no will or life of her own? If her life and will do not exist, then the giving of herself fully to our Lord Jesus Christ is prevented or obstructed. Those who are not allowed to have a relationship, an opinion, an expression, a life, or a heart of their own will be hindered in entering into a personal relationship with the Lord because it is in the Lord's name that they are told they do not exist. "The Lord is my shepherd" is taken out of their reach by those proclaiming the dominion of males, which then results in abuse, enslavement, and a rationale for men to fulfill their desires for power and the gratification of their own flesh.

What about daughters who do ask questions and have formed some opinions of their own? Well, predictably, there are some places where fundamentalist and patriarchal families can send their daughters for "rehab." The Hephzibah House is one of them. It is an oasis for those wishing to put females "in their place" as subservient to men (Jeri Masse has an audio presentation at www.jeriwho.net/tlohh.html; cf., formerhephzibahgirls.webs.com).

Patriarchy highlights the human obsession with having power, control and dominion over others. "Why does there always have to be one who is more powerful" than others (*CAI*, p.60)? "The most powerful are constantly trying to overstep the personal boundaries of the others" (*CAI*, p.151).

"Powerful figures are often aware that the erogenous zones are a significant part of one's identity. That is the reason these areas have been used to oppress people for centuries. History and current events give abundant examples of this. A substantial amount of torture involves injuring people sexually, either by using physical or mental violence" (*CAI*, pp.173-174). "Women's ability to experience their own sexuality is taken from them" in many places in the world by "female circumcision" (*CAI*, p.174).

The practice of males "ruling over" women appeared as a result of sin entering into the world. Before Adam and Eve's disobedience, their relationship was one of *oneness* and *mutuality*. "The two will become one." The Lord gave "them" dominion over the earth. They were partners in God's work. The power struggles that are expressed in "gender wars" occur because of sin. Redemption in Christ brings both sexes together to labor in Jesus' kingdom.

Men's Power Over Women Is Propagated and Enforced by Religious Leaders. "Church leaders have more power than ordinary Christians. They can stimulate or delay change. Because of their powerful position, they are more responsible…for the impact of oppressive systems" (*CAI*, pp.285-286). When a girl in a church was made pregnant by an American during the war, a pastor forbade her to enter the sanctuary. A survivor noted, "That was how everyone knew that she had to get married. That's how powerful the pastor was" (*CAI*, p.59). The church, according to one survivor, "gives people no say in matters, and keeps them dependent" (*CAI*, p.267).

Patriarchy largely sees the value of a woman in terms of her uterus. "Patriarchal religions thus demonstrate that a woman is not allowed to have a will of her own. She serves only for reproduction" (*CAI*, p.174). There is a huge emphasis in the patriarchy movement on the necessity of having a "quiver full" of children. The worth of a wife—whether consciously or unconsciously—is judged by how many babies she brings forth.

Such teaching flagrantly denies the New Testament teaching that *singleness is a godly option for men and women in Christ's kingdom.* The Christian patriarchy movement assumes that a daughter will remain in the family until her father selects a husband for her. That is why they deny advanced education to girls. Singleness is ruled out by their Old Testament-based theology.

And how do couples who cannot have children fare in this system? They feel condemned because a full quiver is not forthcoming. The implication often is that there must be some sin in their life that is blocking conception.

Patriarchy illustrates the very real danger of using the Bible as justification for an ungodly power-hungry agenda. When certain Biblical verses are used out of context, "we give men the right to view women as their possessions and do with them as they wish. Men who want to keep women subordinate to them can read and interpret the Bible in such a way that demonstrates their right. They abuse the Bible, using God to legitimate their misconduct toward women and girls" (*CAI*, p.222).

Patriarchy endorses, even encourages male access to multiple females beyond the wife. History abundantly shows that many manifestations of patriarchy are accompanied with *polygamy*—a man having more than one woman. *Christianity & Incest* documents the connection between the hierarchical/patriarchal view of men and women and male relatives using this church-sanctioned perspective as a rationale to violate female family members.

Though he did not mean to sanction sexual misbehavior by fathers, Voddie Baucham—a person in demand as a speaker at home school events—nevertheless utters words that would send shivers down the spines of the incest survivors in the Netherlands who were interviewed in *Christianity & Incest*.

A lot of men are leaving their wives for younger women because they yearn for attention from younger women. And God gave them a daughter who can give them that. And instead, they go find a substitute daughter, You've seen it! We've all seen it! These OLD GUYS! Going and finding substitute daughters. Why? Why? We don't understand what love is, folks (http://web.me.com/voddieb/vbm/Blog/Entries/2009/11/19_November_Question_of_the_Month_[Updated_Edition]).

One of the central teachings of the Christian patriarchy movement instructs parents how to have their daughters "give their hearts to their fathers." "Melissa Keen, 25, helps put on Vision Forum's annual Father-Daughter Retreat, an event that's described on Vision Forum's website in terms that are, in a word, discomfiting—'*He leads her, woos her, and wins her with a tenderness and affection unique to the bonds of father and daughter*'" (newsfeed.time.com/2010/12/08/meet-the-selfless-women-of-the-stay-at-home-daughters-movement).

Stacy McDonald in her book, *Raising Maidens of Virtue*, describes in vivid detail a ceremony where daughters give small charms to their fathers as a symbol of their virginity. The father, then, is to be their "kingly defender" and the keeper of their virginity. The virgin's heart is to be set on the dad and the relationship with him is most important. The McDonalds have 163 questions they ask of any potential suitor. A video of the reception at the wedding of their daughter shows Mr. McDonald taking the charm given to him by her, handing it over to the groom, and saying, "I give you my daughter's heart."

Cindy Kunsman on her blog has referred to this type of father-daughter interaction as "emotional incest" (botkinsyndrome.blogspot.com/search/label/Botkin%20Syndrome). Needless to say, there is nothing in the Bible about a requirement for daughters to give their hearts to their fathers. Our heart is to be the possession of the Lord alone.

The Christian patriarchy movement is very dogmatic that daughters being at home and serving their fathers is the "godly and biblical" way and that anything outside of this is "ungodly and unbiblical." And yet the Word of God is silent about this matter.

THE WIFE IN THE PRESENCE OF HER HUSBAND AS A LITTLE GIRL

The late Helen Andelin's *Fascinating Womanhood* appeared in 1963, and was quite influential in the emerging home school movement from the 1970s onwards. Her thoughts on a wife being "childlike" are fascinating in light of the patterns of abuse uncovered in *Christianity & Incest.*

> To accentuate youthfulness in dress, visit young girls' shops....There you will see buttons and bows, checks, plaids, pleats, stripes, jumpers, daisies, and even satin, lace, and velvet. All of their clothes are pretty....Little girls wear ribbons, bows, barrettes, and flowers in their hair. And they wear cute little hats.....There are a few women who resist the idea of acting childlike, who consider it an insult to their good sense for anyone to expect them to act the part of a little girl. They insist on believing that really sensible men, the kind they admire, would be repulsed instead of attracted to a childlike creature. The only way to prove to yourself if childlikeness is charming to men is to try it in your own life to test your husband's reaction....When a woman matures there's a marked tendency for her to lose this childlike trait, especially when she gets married. She somehow feels that now she must grow up completely. Truly fascinating women always remain somewhat little girls, regardless of age. (*Fascinating Womanhood*, pp. 342-344).

It would be interesting to know Helen's take on polygamy in light of the Mormonism she embraced, which historically condoned the practice of men having multiple wives.

It is important to keep in mind the perverted use of "honor your father and mother" as a rationale for males to have access to their wives and to their female relatives. The incest survivors "honored their fathers and mothers, despite the sexual abuse by their fathers" (*CAI*, p.195).

Patriarchy predominates in very narrow, sectarian "Christian" practice. As patriarchy comes to expression in the home schooling movement, there is a tendency to have an inbred, tribal approach to relationships. One survivor described her upbringing in the Dutch Reformed church: "The church dictated our entire social life, school, clubs, and acquaintances. Friends were allowed to come home with us as long as they were from the same church. When I left the church, I received a letter telling me that I was damned. My parents dropped me too" (*CAI*, p.70).

Many in Christian patriarchy are advocating the Family Integrated Church movement. A lot of parents pursue this to ensure that their children will only be able to associate with "like-minded" (their often-used phrase) families (cf., Wade Burleson, http://kerussocharis.blogspot.com/2008/09/patriarchy-and-family-integrated-church.html, also see: http://www.thatmom.com/?page_id=2675)

DEEP WOUNDING IN AMERICAN PATRIARCHY

An American example of how patriarchy deeply wounded a mother and daughter. The interviews from *Christianity & Incest* were drawn from women's experiences in Holland. Wilma Goolsby-Gibbs gave her testimony in "Excommunicated," one of the essays in *Rape, Incest, Battery: Women Writing Out the Pain* (Miriam K. Harris, ed., TCU Press, 2000, pp.46-53). Notice how these excerpts precisely parallel the main points that surfaced in the research shared in *Christianity & Incest.*

- **Church-going people:** She and her husband were immersed in church activities.

- **Husband was a church leader:** Her husband "was a minister of the church."

- **Husband raped daughter:** Her husband sexually abused a fifteen-year old daughter, and he physically and emotionally abused the mother and the other children.

- **Husband paraded "male headship":** The husband used his alleged patriarchal authority to get his way: "I'm the head of this house and you will obey me!"

- **"Obey" parents twisted:** One "particular elder repeatedly told my daughter face-to-face that she had to obey her father."

- **Child thought incest is normal:** "At one time she thought all dads did it to their daughters."

- **Child blackmailed/threatened:** When the daughter wanted to tell mom what was going on, "he told her if she did it would kill me. He said I would have a heart attack and die."

- **Victims not taken seriously:** When the mom and the children went to "the pastor and his wife, and another minister in the church...they told me point blank that they thought we were lying about a man of God." "Every time I tried to get their help, they refused me."

- **Child blamed for adult's behavior:** "Another minister said that if Jack was abusing Alice or committing incest, she was as much to blame as her dad. In other words…he was going to blame the child and not the responsible adult."

- **Those in power sided with the abuser:** Now the mother and kids "were being rejected" and the abuser was defended by the church leaders. In the end, the mother was "excommunicated" and the husband's responsibilities in the church continued.

- **Child's pain continues long after the trauma:** The daughter "continued to suffer for something she had not been responsible for."

- **The abuser continues as church leader:** "As far as our perpetrator was concerned, he was given more sermons to preach, more pats on the back and a cooler full of meat when I obtained a protective order against him."

PATRIARCHY PROVIDES FERTILE SOIL FOR MISTREATMENT OF WOMEN IN UNTOLD WAYS.

Christian churches have been violating fundamental human rights in this way for centuries, particularly women's right to freedom of opinion. They have chosen the side of the dominant group in society: domineering men. The result is that they have legitimated and stimulated the denial of and contempt for women by propagating this morality to men and women. Christian churches did not propagate this morality with the intent to stimulate men to sexually abuse girls in their (immediate) family, but sexual abuse of girls is the ultimate consequence of a church-propagated morality which devalues women and makes them inferior to men (*CAI*, pp.275-276).

Patriarchy perverts the original creation of male and female. It must be underscored that the most basic issue in the male/female relationship is expressed in Paul's words in Ephesians 5:32, "This is a profound mystery—but I am talking about Christ and the church."

The most fundamental problem with sexual deviations is that they mar, violate and contradict in various ways the beauty and purity of Jesus' relationship with his Bride, the *ekklesia*.... [They] are all destructive perversions of "the beginning" when God created them male and female, and of the "fullness of time" when Christ came to gather a Bride from all the nations (Jon Zens, *What's With Paul & Women?*

Unlocking the Cultural Background to 1 Timothy 2, Ekklesia Press, 2010, p. 115).

We know that nothing was made without Jesus Christ. In the beginning the Lord made "Adam." The very word itself embraces male and female—"When God created Adam, he made Adam in the likeness of God. He created them male and female and blessed them. And when they were created, he called them 'Adam'" (Gen. 5:2).

Eve was "in" Adam before they became separate entities, and they were still "one flesh" after she was taken out of him. Adam was the "source" of Eve, just as Jesus is the "source" of the Bride—he is the vine, we are the branches. This is the first earthly picture of Christ and his Bride. You can read Genesis 1-2 over and over again, and you will never find the key tenet of patriarchy—that Adam was given "authority over" Eve before the fall into sin. They were created as equals—they were both partners in carrying out dominion over the earth (not over each other!).

That Eve is called an "ezer" ("one with strength") does not help the patriarchy case. Traditionally, "ezer" has been assumed to mean "helper," "assistant," taken to imply that Adam is "above" her in some way. But since this Hebrew word is most often used of the

Lord as the "strength" of Israel, it lends no weight to the opinion that Eve exists as one subservient to her husband (*cf.*, http://www.clarksons.org/articles/GenesisHelper.htm; www.cbeinternational.org/?q=content/genesis-1-3; newlife.id.au/equality-and.../a-suitable-helper-in-the-septuagint/).

Thus any view of women that renders them as a group which exists solely for the benefit of males is grossly out of touch with the truth as it is in Jesus. Patriarchy as an ideology camps around the Old Covenant, ignores the functioning of women that existed even in Israel, and is blind to the blossoming of female ministry that is revealed in the pages of the New Testament. Contemporary Christian patriarchy has invented a number of rules regarding male/female relationships, designated them as "the godly way," and condemned others who will not toe the line with their self-imposed standards.

"According to a study of the University of Pennsylvania School of Medicine, up to thirty-three percent of American girls are molested" (Marianne Williamson, "A Course on Weight Loss," audio book, CD #3, track 5). Even if actual sexual contact is almost non-existent in today's Christian patriarchy movement, the fact remains that deep emotional damage has been done and will continue to be done to many girls and young women whose existence is absorbed into the male species. As I see it, one of the worst outcomes of patriarchy is that daughters grow up being taught the Bible in such a way that they can only see themselves in relation to men, beings "in relation to others" (*CAI*, p.140). Such women end up feeling like a "being without a soul, a puppet on a string" (*CAI*, p.253). They are not accepted as "thinking human beings" but viewed "as an extension of their husbands [and fathers] and existing for the benefit of their husbands [and fathers]" (*CAI*, p.255).

Certainly there are young ladies and moms who seem to flourish in Christian patriarchy—but that is only because they function within the acceptable boundaries of the male-defined patriarchal box. I've seen interviews with women who live in polygamous families. Many of them say they "love it," and are doing just fine as human beings. Just because some people appear to be happy and content in a closed system is no indication that they are in reality experiencing a life that is in line with all of their potential as defined by the Lord. Living a lie long enough, you can appear to be having a great time in it.

A final word to women who have been hurt by patriarchy. My guess is that a number of women who read this book will find themselves saying, "That's exactly what happened to me when I was growing up!" For some, reading these pages will be extremely painful. Dan Kimball wrote a book that expresses a truth that many in our culture need to hear—*They Like Jesus But Not the Church*. A lot of things passed off as "truth" by church leaders have nothing to do with Jesus—and patriarchy is one of them. Jesus is about *life* and *loving relationships* flowing out of his life in us. Religion is about totem poles of authority, about chain-of-command, about somebody being over somebody else, and about power-brokers putting the wills of others out of business. Jesus, however, said "No" to all of this.

> You know that the Gentile rulers lord it over them, and their great men exercise authority over them. It is not so among you, but whoever wishes to become great among you shall be your servant, and whoever wishes to be first among you shall be your slave (Matthew 20:25-27)…. But do not be called Rabbi, for One is your teacher, and you are all brothers and sisters…. And do not be called leaders, for One is your leader, that is Christ. But the greatest among you will be your servant (Matthew 23:8-11).

A lot of church leaders and Bible-teachers are putting heavy burdens on women. But Jesus said,

"Come to me, all who are weary and heavy-laden, and I will give you rest [Sabbath]. Take my yoke upon you, and learn from me, for I am gentle and humble in heart, and you will find rest [Sabbath] for your souls. For my yoke is easy and my load is light" (Matthew 11:28-30). Patriarchy puts women in bondage; Jesus sets the captives free.

If patriarchy has brought you to this kind of heart-cry—"I have been denied as a person; I have no will of my own; my identity has been negated; I have always felt like a thing; I have been told to suppress my own desires and feelings; I have only been allowed to be the way others wanted me to be; I have no say in matters; I cannot ask any questions; I have been told not to use my imagination"—I would encourage you to find your way out of its grip with the help of Jesus Christ, and others who will come along side of you. As Yogi Berra once said, "When you arrive at a fork in the road—take it."

OTHER SOURCES
Further reading on this subject

Sandra L. Bem, "Traditional Male/Female Roles Promote Sexual Violence," *Sexual Violence: Opposing Viewpoints*. Bruno Leone, ed., Greenhaven Press, 1997, pp.40-43.

Margaret L. Bendroth, "Fundamentalism & Femininity: Points of Encounter Between Religious Conservatives & Women, 1919-1935," *American Church History: A Reader*, Henry W. Bowden & P.C. Kemeny, eds., Abingdon Press, 1998, pp.230-240.

Anil Bordia, et al., eds., "Why Are Girls Still Held Back?" *Gender & Education for All: The Leap to Equality*, Unesco Publishing, 2003, pp. 115-153.

Lisa Sowle Cahill, *Between the Sexes: Foundations for a Christian Ethic of Sexuality*, Fortress Press, 1985, 166pp.

Karen Campbell, Podcasts: Patriarchy and Patriocentricity Series One 2007, http://www.thatmom.com/?page_id=2659 / Patriarchy and Patriocentricity Series Two 2010, http://www.thatmom.com/?page_id=5036

Gospel for Asia, "Beauty for Ashes: The Fragile Existence of Many Asian Women," *Searching Together*, 32:4, 2004.

J. Lee Grady, 10 *Lies Men Believe*, Charisma House, 2011, 240pp.

Stanton L. Jones, "How to Teach Sex: Seven Realities that Christians in Every Congregation Need to Know," *Christianity Today*, January, 2011, pp.35-39.

Kathryn Joyce, *Quiverfull: Inside the Christian Patriarchy Movement*, Beacon Press, 2009, 272pp.

Charles Kimball, *When Religion Becomes Evil*, Harper, 2002, 240pp.

Nicholas Kristof & Sheryl WuDunn, *Half the Sky: Turning Oppression into Opportunity for Women*, Random House, 2009, 320pp.

Lewis Wells, http://thecommandmentsofmen. blogspot.com/2011/02/daughters-shaving-daddies-i-wish-i-were.html#more

Hillary McFarland, *Quivering Daughters: Hope & Healing for the Daughters of Patriarchy*, Darklight Press, 2010, 270pp.

Lisa Graham McMinn, *Growing Strong Daughters: Encouraging Girls to Become All They're Meant to Be*, Baker, 2007, 208pp.

Maria Mies, *Patriarchy & Accumulation On a World Scale: Women in the International Division of Labor*, Zed Books, 2nd edition, 1999.

Russell D. Moore, "After Patriarchy, What? Why Egalitarians Are Winning the Gender Debate," *Journal of the Evangelical Theological Society*, 49:3, September, 2006, pp.569-576.

Clark Morphew & Linda Kohl, "Women Hold to Biblical Role of Submission," "Leader Expects Obedience from His People," *Christ's Household: Faith & Fear*, a multi-part series in the *St. Paul Dispatch*, July, 1984.

Doug Phillips, www.visionforumministries.org/issues/family/the_patriarchy_paradigm.

Howard A. Snyder with Daniel V. Runyon, "From Male Leadership to Male/Female Partnership," *Foresight: 10 Major Trends that Will Affect the Future of Christians and the Future*, Thomas Nelson Publishers, 1986, pp.95-110.

Jon Zens, "Moses & the Millennium: An Appraisal of Christian Reconstructionism," *Searching Together*, 17:2-4, 1988, 52pp.

Jon Zens, *What's With Paul & Women? Unlocking the Cultural Background to 1 Timothy 2*, Ekklesia Press, 2010.

APPENDIX

One Brother's Experience with Patriarchy
by Stephen Crosby, North Carolina

Thomas Aquinas (1225-1274) said regarding women:

As regards the individual nature, woman is defective and misbegotten, for the active power of the male seed tends to the production of a perfect likeness in the masculine sex; while the production of a woman comes from defect in the active power.

As awful as this is, it is not a unique sentiment in the annals of Christian history. The prejudice goes further back than Aquinas, even to the Garden—"the woman you gave me...." Much "Christian doctrine" regarding women is actually pagan in its roots. More disturbing than the past history are the contemporary variants of the same root ignorance in modern Evangelical Fundamentalism. The following accounts are true. What follows is only a short list of the fruit of fundamentalist patriarchy that I have experienced over a broad spectrum of the Evangelical church. Names have been withheld for privacy reasons.

- My own daughter spent a year in a young people's discipleship training intensive sort of thing. She was a fine young girl, sexually pure, passionate for God. But because her goals were not related to being a missionary or to marry someone who was going to be a "five-folder," she was overtly and covertly rejected by peers and "leaders." She wanted to go into business. She was viewed with great suspicion. It was so bad that the group thought she, as well as Rita and myself, needed "deliverance" for being so "marginally spiritual" and "lacking in discernment." The final heartbreak came when the "father-apostle" of this group would not write her a letter of recommendation to go to college. It broke her heart.

- The same group (as do many others) taught against birth control. Women were baby factories. Based on "full-quiver" teaching, women were to marry young and pump out babies as fast as they can.

- The same group (and others) did not believe that women should get an education, as they should be "keepers at home."

- The same group (as do others) taught

dogmatically and aggressively that a "godly marriage" is based on a woman leaving her family and cleaving to her husband. When I pointed out that the exact opposite is to be found in Genesis (it is the husband that leaves and cleaves) they stood there with their mouths literally hanging open. When I challenged them to show me scripturally where their belief system came from, here's the gem of an exegetical response I received: "We get it from somewhere." Exact wording. No repentance. Rigid entrenchment of culturally baseless gender bias.

- Same group as above, when their young people's discipleship group would do their cross nation tour, they would make all the girls get off the bus at a gas station/rest stop before the boys, go in and turn around all the covers of the porn magazines, before the boys were allowed in the store to use the rest room, lest they be "defiled."

- Same group as above: if a boy expressed normal interest in a girl he would often be made to feel unclean (see rest-stop story above). When this group thankfully imploded, a disproportionately high number of young men in the discipleship group turned to homosexuality. If you make a boy feel filthy for even thinking about a girl, what do you expect? A train wreck, of course.

- Same group: any young woman who was attractive was suspect as being *de-facto* sexually unclean by the group leaders. One time an attractive young girl on the bus was not allowed off to use the bathroom until she "confessed" what the group leader believed had been "revealed" to him about the young girl's "secret" lust. She did not know what the leader was talking about. The leader refused to let her off the bus. She literally pooped in her pants and had a nervous breakdown. What wonderful kingdom ministry.

- When I tried to present the problems to various leaders I was told that the victims of these treatments: "Just need to forgive, and get over it," "they have a Jezebel spirit," "They have a problem with authority," "They have a root of bitterness," etc.

- Just get over it, huh? That is like asking a survivor of Auschwitz to "just get over it."

- When I tried to bring remediation to this group I was roundly resisted, marginalized, and accused of trying to take over, of stealing the "father-apostle's" mantle.

- I am aware of Vision Forum (I used to have their product catalog) where they teach their boys to be "knights in shining armor" and their women are supposed to be fair damsels in distress, passive, waiting for the boys/men to rescue them. This is such stone ignorance—as if medieval chivalry is the standard for the kingdom of God. Medieval chivalry is a myth, not far from la Cosa Nostra in its ethics. It was basically a thin veneer of morality used to justify the unrestrained behavior of the nobility to help themselves to whatever they wanted at the expense of the peasantry. Some patriarchs are not content turning the clock back to the 1950s. They want to turn it back to the Middle Ages, all in a passion to "return to Godly standards" of gender roles.

- The same group as above insists that only the Geneva Bible is the authorized word of God as it is the one the Pilgrims used. Yes, those good tobacco smoking, beer drinking, dancing, and partying Pilgrims! Patriarchal, fundamentalist, rubbish.

- I know of churches that make women leave the room when the men have to talk about "church things."

- I know of another situation where a man forbade his wife or daughters from reading the Scriptures based on an ignorant understanding of "the Scriptures are given to a man to profit thereby, KJV." This man actually had his 13-year-old son read the Scriptures to his mother and sisters. He also forbade his wife to vote (that would be giving a woman authority over a man) and would not let her speak or sing in the church without his permission. He also had been pressuring his wife for years for polygamy.

Acknowledgements:

I would like to thank the following people for their invaluable gifts and input that helped shape the final form of this project—Wilma Bell, Wade Burleson, Karen Campbell, Gordon Gillesby, Kathy Huff, Bonnie Jaeckle, Ralph Polendo, Timothy L. Price, Jodi Root….

and Yogi Berra.

ℰ𝓅 *Ekklesia Press*

Ekklesia Press offers books to develop and encourage believers to be God's Ekklesia: His called out who live within an unbelieving world. Our productions have a prophetic edge. They will challenge you, uproot empty tradition and help you to live the kingdom of God in conjunction to others who realize the Kingdom of God is not just an eventuality.

The Diluted Church
Calling Believers To Live Out Of Their True Heritage
by Timothy L. Price *(June 2005)*

The Diluted Church is extremely salient in a politically charged world. It challenge how you think about yourself and the usual tendency toward a var of allegiances rather than one. If you think either side of the political aisle a with God's purposes this book will help expose the error of playing some else's game according to their rules. You will see that God can be represe without wrapping Him in a political, nationalistic or idealistic cloak define people and ideals that have nothing to do with Him.

Christ in Y'all
Following Jesus Into Community
by Neil Carter *(August 2008)*

This book is based from the text in Colossians, "Christ in you the hop glory." The "you" really means a collective you: as in a group. God inter to make His home within the community of believers. Life as a followe Jesus was never meant to be lived alone. Hearing God speak and follov his voice are for a "we" rather than a "me." This books offers key elemen having a thriving Christian community. *Christ in Y'all* gives practical insi into surviving the pitfalls of home-based fellowships.

NEW THIS YEAR!

The Spirituality of Discontent
Reflections on the Sermon on the Mount
By Bong Manayon *(due out: Spring 2011)*

The Spirituality of Discontent is a pastoral work written originally to the aut son Khalil. Bong Manayon, a retired Filipino pastor, expounds upon the Ser on the Mount in a way his son, and everyone, can understand. He uses s indigenous language of the Philippines to flesh out meaning behind Ch words that are not so clear in English. This book is inspiring and upliftin it challenges the reader. Manayon gives a unique delivery to perhaps the n fundamental of Christ's teaching.

First impressions can mislead us
For we do not Know the heart
We can often be mistaken
Since we only Know in part -
Fitzhugh
11 Co - 5:16 - Regard no one
according to the Flesh "